Harriet Tubman
THE ROAD TO FREEDOM

By Rae Bains and Joanne Mattern
Illustrated by Larry Johnson

SCHOLASTIC INC.
New York   Toronto   London   Auckland   Sydney
Mexico City   New Delhi   Hong Kong   Buenos Aires

ISBN-13: 978-0-439-83251-9
ISBN-10: 0-439-83251-9

Copyright © 2006 by Scholastic Inc.

12 11 10 9 8 7 6 5 4 3 2 1   7 8 9 10 11/0

Printed in the U.S.A.   23

First printing, January 2006

CONTENTS

CHAPTER 1:
Born Into Slavery

It was beautiful along the eastern shore of Maryland's Chesapeake Bay. The waters were filled with fish, oysters, and clams. In the woods lived rabbits, woodchucks, muskrats, deer, and squirrels. Corn, tobacco, wheat, and vegetables grew in the rich soil.

Maryland was a fine place to live during the early 1800s — if you were free. Ben Ross and Harriet Green were not. They were the slaves of a plantation owner named Edward Brodess.

They worked in his fields, cut his lumber, and were his house servants. They did anything he ordered them to do. And their children did the same.

Slaves were chattel. That meant they were pieces of property, like sheep or furniture or bales of cotton. The slaves knew that they could be sold at any time. They knew that their children could be taken from them and sent far, far away, and that they could be beaten or whipped. And they knew that their masters would never be punished because slaves had no rights. They were not allowed any kind of education; they were not even allowed to attend church.

This was the sort of world into which Harriet Ross was born, around 1820. Her exact birthday was never recorded. Her parents could not read or write, and because Harriet was a slave, her master didn't bother to write down the exact date of her birth. She was the fifth of nine

children born to Ben Ross and Harriet Green. They all lived in a tiny, one-room shack. It had a dirt floor, no windows, and no furniture.

There were no beds. The whole family slept on rags and straw spread on the floor. There were no dishes. The slaves' food — mostly corn mush — was eaten right from the pot it was cooked in. They would scoop it out with a piece of flat stone or an oyster shell. And when they ate, they had to stand or sit on the hard ground.

Edward Brodess had a large plantation where he grew apples, wheat, rye, and corn. He also sold timber from forests on the plantation. Harriet's father spent most of his time cutting down trees to be sold to the shipyards in Baltimore, on the other side of Chesapeake Bay. Harriet's mother worked as a servant in the house.

Mr. Brodess had another way to make money. He sold slaves. Whenever any of the Brodesses' slaves had a baby, the child was automatically the Brodesses' property. When the child was old enough to work, Mr. Brodess usually sold him or her. Slave traders from the Deep South often came to the Brodess plantation to buy slaves. During her childhood, Harriet saw many of her brothers, sisters, and friends sold to these traders. She never expected to see them again.

Slave children had almost no time to play. They were put to work as soon as possible, to "earn their keep." When Harriet was still a very small child, she began running errands for Mr. Brodess and his family. She carried messages as

far as ten miles away. She had to go over back roads, through woods, and along riverbanks.

The only tenderness in Harriet's life came from her family. They gave her so much love that she always had something wonderful to hold on to, even at the worst of times. And one day — many years later — Harriet would thank her parents in the best way she could. She would rescue them, plus six of her brothers and one sister, from slavery, taking them north to freedom.

Soon after she turned five, Harriet was given a new task. Mrs. Brodess put her to work in the mansion, called the big house. There were two kinds of slaves on most large plantations. Some slaves worked in the house. These slaves learned special skills. They worked as cooks, maids, and housekeepers. Some slaves cared for children, while others brought food to the table and served guests at parties. House slaves were generally treated much better than field slaves. They wore nicer clothes, and had better food — and more of it — than field slaves. Some even slept in the big house, in case they were needed during the night to help their master's family.

However, most field slaves never set foot inside the big house. They were always outside planting and harvesting crops, caring for animals, and doing other hard, physical work. Field slaves lived in tiny slave quarters. Living conditions there were very hard. Even animals had better quarters than most of the slaves.

When Harriet went to work at the big house as a little girl, she didn't know a thing about housework. She had never even been inside a real house before — only in the one-room slave shacks. And to make things worse, nobody showed her how to do the things she was supposed to do in the mansion.

So it was no surprise when Harriet made all kinds of mistakes. And when she made mistakes, she was punished.

CHAPTER 2:
Hired Out

When Harriet was six, she was sent to live with the Cooks, a family of weavers. Their home was many miles from the Brodess plantation. Harriet hated being so far from her family. But the Brodesses wanted her to learn weaving. Then she would be able to weave for the Brodess family. So, like it or not, Harriet went.

Life with the Cooks was no better than it had been on the Brodess plantation. But Harriet did not stay long with the Cooks. She proved to be a slow weaver, so Mrs. Cook turned Harriet over to her husband. One day, even though she was very sick with measles, Mr. Cook sent her down to the river. She was told to check his muskrat traps. To do this, she had to wade through ice-cold, fast-flowing waters in her bare feet, wearing only a thin shirt.

The next day, Harriet began to shake and cough. Soon she was burning with fever

O well

and could not do any work. She lay in a corner, feeling terrible. Word of her illness quickly passed from one slave to the next, until it reached Harriet's mother.

She begged Mr. Brodess to bring her little girl home. Mr. Brodess agreed. He didn't want to pay the Cooks for teaching someone who was too sick to learn anything, and the Cooks didn't want a slave who couldn't work. So he had Harriet brought home. There, her mother nursed the little girl back to health.

For Harriet's next job, Mrs. Brodess hired her out to look after another family's baby. Here is how Harriet talked about it years later: "I was only seven years old when I was sent to take care of the baby. I was so little I had to sit on the floor and have the baby put in my lap. And that baby was always in my lap except when it was asleep or its mother was feeding it."

Handling such a big responsibility was hard for young Harriet. She never had any time to play or be by herself. She was constantly watched by her new mistress, and she was very strict with her. If she misbehaved, Harriet knew she would be given a whipping. This kind of punishment was used all the time. The owners wanted to keep their slaves frightened. They did not want the slaves to speak up or fight back — or try to escape.

CHAPTER 3:
Rebellion!

The owners could not break the spirit of the slaves. There always were slaves who stood up for their rights. They bravely held religious services, even though that was forbidden. They studied reading and writing in secret. They hid and fed other slaves who were trying to escape to the North.

And every year, there were slave uprisings. The plantation owners tried to keep the news of these revolts from getting out. They didn't want their own slaves to hear about them and do the same thing. But word still passed from

one slave to another, from one plantation to another, all over the South. It didn't matter that the owners said the slaves were content. The slaves knew better.

From the time she was a baby, Harriet listened to the stories of slaves fighting back. She heard of a slave named Gabriel Prosser. In 1800, Prosser had planned a great rebellion. Several slaves were ready to march with him. But he was stopped at the last moment, when a traitor told several slave owners about the rebellion.

Harriet also heard of Denmark Vesey, who preached that all people were equal. Vesey was a free black man who had once been a slave. He was also the leader of thousands of slaves living in South Carolina. Vesey's group was ready to rise up in the name of freedom on July 14, 1822. But his plans, like those of Gabriel Prosser, were told to slave owners by frightened servants, and he was stopped.

Harriet heard of other uprisings—large and small—taking place in many parts of the South. All this meant one thing to the young girl— she was not the only angry slave in America. *Someday,* she told herself, *I'm going to be free! And when that day comes, I'm going to help bring others to freedom.*

Harriet did not hide her feelings. She spoke out fearlessly to the other slaves on the plantation. And she refused to smile or make believe she was happy in front of the Brodess family.

CHAPTER 4:
Family Strength

Harriet's mother was worried about her. If Harriet angered Mr. Brodess or his wife, they might sell Harriet "down the river." Selling someone down the river meant selling that person to a slave trader. The trader would take his new slave down to the Deep South to be put to work in the rice or cotton fields. Life was hard for a slave in Maryland. But it was ten times harder in the Deep South.

Mrs. Brodess did not like Harriet's proud, defiant looks. She decided to break the child's spirit. To do so, she hired out the nine-year-old girl to another family in the county. These people made her work all day, cleaning house. Then she had to work at night, caring for a baby. For no reason, she was punished every day. And she was fed only enough food to keep her alive.

After a while, Harriet was little more than skin and bones. She was not able to work anymore. Now, sure that she was "broken," the family sent Harriet back to the Brodess plantation. Her body was weak and weary, but not her spirit. That was still strong.

Harriet's parents did their best to help her get well. Her mother cared for her every free moment she had. And her father, Ben, taught her all kinds of amazing and useful things. Even though he had never gone to school, Ben was a very wise man. He knew a lot about nature. He could tell that it would be a hard winter when the animals grew thicker coats in the fall. He knew where the fishing was good. And he knew which wild plants were safe to eat. As soon as Harriet was feeling better, he took her on Sunday-afternoon walks in the woods and along the river.

Part of Harriet's strength came from her brothers and sisters. After a day of working in the fields under a boiling sun, they came back

to the shack. They brought her all the news of the day. They sang songs. They told stories. They told jokes to make her laugh. They did everything they could to make their little sister happy.

Another part of Harriet's strength came from her faith. The slaves were not allowed to have a real church. But they were very religious and held services every Sunday morning. On every plantation there usually was at least one slave who could read or knew the Bible very well. And all the other slaves learned Bible stories and prayers from this person.

Music was also an important part of the slaves' life. The slaves often sang while they worked. Music was a big part of their church services as well. The slaves sang songs called spirituals that spoke about heroes and events from the Bible.

Of all the stories in the Bible, the one the slaves liked most was about Moses. He had led the Israelites from slavery. One of the most popular spirituals was about Moses, and included the lines, "Go down, Moses, way down in Egypt's land. Tell old Pharaoh, 'Let my people go.'" The slaves prayed for a Moses of their own, someone who would lead them to freedom.

Harriet believed deeply that the burden on her people would be eased. She believed that they were meant to be free. She believed what the Bible said: All people were equal in the eyes of God.

CHAPTER 5:

As Strong as a Man

In the next three years, Harriet grew stronger in body and faith. Mr. Brodess felt she was too surly and caused too much trouble to be a house slave. Mr. Brodess hired her out to another master who had her do work hard enough for a grown man. She split rails with an ax, hauled wood, and did other heavy jobs. It was difficult but she never gave up, even when it seemed too much to bear.

By the time she was eleven, Harriet was muscular and very strong. She could work as hard and as long as any grown-up. Mr. Brodess saw

this and put her to work in the fields. Like all the other women in the fields, Harriet wore a bandanna—a large handkerchief—on her head. For the rest of her life, she would always wear a bandanna. It was to remind her of her days as a slave, and how far she had come from the fields.

Harriet preferred working in the fields to working in the house. It was good to be away from the sharp eyes of the mistresses, and it was even better to be out in the fresh air. Harriet also liked the fact that the work made her body strong and muscular. She was proud that she could do the same work as a man.

CHAPTER 6:

An Underground Railroad

In 1831, new, harsher laws were passed. Now, slaves were not supposed to talk while they worked. They were never to be on the public roads without a pass from their masters. And the old rules were made stricter. All of this happened because of an uprising led by a man named Nat Turner.

Nat Turner was a slave from Virginia. In the summer of 1831, Turner—called the Prophet—led about seventy slaves in a bloody revolt. It took armed troops to stop the revolt, and three full months to capture Turner.

The slave owners were scared. If a revolt could happen in Virginia, it could happen anywhere. This fear haunted them more and more. That is why they made stricter laws for the slaves.

Now slaves were forbidden to gather in large groups. It also became illegal for anyone to teach a slave to read or write. Despite these laws, slaves continued to meet secretly and dream of a way to get to freedom.

Nat Turner had lit the flame of rebellion in many slaves. Harriet was one of them. "I feel just like Nat Turner did," she said one night to her family. "It's better to be dead than a slave."

"It's better to be alive and free," said her brother William.

"And how do we get that?" Harriet asked him. "You know Mr. Brodess won't ever give us our freedom."

"I'm not talking about what he gives," William told her. "I'm talking about what we take for ourselves — like a ride to freedom on the Underground Railroad."

"What's that?" Harriet wanted to know.

William told Harriet the story of Tice Davids. Mr. Davids was a slave in Kentucky who ran away. When the plantation owner found out that Mr. Davids was gone, he set out after him. Mr. Davids swam across the Ohio River with the owner rowing close behind. By the time the owner's boat landed, there was no trace of Tice Davids. It was as if he had vanished into thin air.

The runaway was being helped by people who hated slavery. But the plantation owner only knew that he had vanished. When the slave owner returned, he told everybody that "Tice Davids disappeared so fast, he must have gone on an underground road."

This story was repeated again and again. Soon slaves were talking about the wonderful secret passage to freedom. Of course, there was no

underground road or tunnel from the South to the North. But the slaves kept telling the story anyway. It gave them hope.

It was around this time that the first railroads were being built in the United States. Trains were the fastest way of traveling that anyone had ever seen. The slaves heard about the railroads. Soon, people were talking about the "Underground Railroad" that took runaway slaves quickly and safely to the North.

This had nothing to do with trains and underground tunnels. The truth was that there were good people who risked their lives to help slaves escape. Some of them hid runaways in their cellars, barns, attics, or in secret rooms in their houses.

These brave people were called stationmasters. The hiding places were called depots or stations. Other people took the runaways from one depot to another in a hay wagon, on horseback, or by foot. These people were called con-

ductors. The runaways themselves were known as passengers or parcels. A child was a small parcel, and a grown-up was a large parcel.

After William told Harriet about the Underground Railroad, she thought about it all the time. She found out that some white people in the area were helping runaway slaves. Most of these people belonged to a religious group called Quakers. Quakers believed that slavery was wrong and did all they could to stop it. But Harriet didn't know enough to risk a ride on the Underground Railroad just yet. Still, she told herself that someday she would take that ride to freedom. Maybe all the slaves would. It was this hope that kept Harriet going.

CHAPTER 7:
Not Worth a Penny

When Harriet was around fifteen, her hope — and her life — almost ended. One September evening she was sent to the village store. While she was there, another slave hurried in. He belonged to a farmer with the last name Barrett. A moment later, Mr. Barrett's overseer, who was in charge of the slaves, rushed in.

"Get back to the field!" the overseer shouted at the slave.

The slave just stared back silently. Nobody else in the store made a move.

"I'll whip you," the overseer threatened.

36

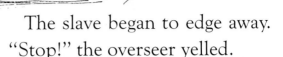

The slave began to edge away. "Stop!" the overseer yelled.

He pointed at Harriet and a young boy next to her. "Hold him, so I can tie him up and whip him."

Harriet didn't obey the order. And she kept the boy from doing anything.

Suddenly, the slave ran to the door. Harriet ran to block the door so the overseer could not follow the slave. The overseer leaped to the store counter and picked up a heavy lead weight. He whirled and threw the weight at the runaway. But it missed the man. The heavy piece of metal struck Harriet in the head. She fell to the floor, unconscious.

Harriet was brought back home. She was so badly hurt that no one expected her to live through the night. All the slaves gathered around to watch over Harriet and pray for her. Harriet's mother prayed and cared for her, too. Harriet lived through the night, but she remained unconscious for many days. Even after she finally woke up, she was very sick.

For the next couple of months, Harriet lay near death. At first, she couldn't eat. She grew thinner and thinner. She slept most of the time. Her wound was healing slowly, but there was a very deep cut in her forehead. It left a scar she would carry for the rest of her life.

Mr. Brodess was sure Harriet was going to die, so he tried to sell her. Time after time, he brought slave buyers to the shack, where Harriet lay on a pile of rags. But each time, the buyer's answer was the same: "Even if she lives, she'll never be able to put in a day's work. I wouldn't give you a penny for her."

Winter came, and Harriet was still alive. Her parents were thankful, but still worried about her. Harriet could walk and talk and do light

chores around the shack. But sometimes, in the
middle of whatever she was doing, Harriet fell
asleep.

It could even happen while she was saying
something. She would simply stop talking, close
her eyes, and sleep for a few minutes. Then she

would wake up and go on talking as if no time had passed.

Harriet also had strange dreams during her "spells." She often dreamed of slaves coming to America in the holds of big ships. Another recurring dream beckoned her to freedom. Harriet later described this dream, saying, "I seemed to see a line, and on the other side of the line were green fields, and lovely flowers, and beautiful white ladies who stretched out their arms to me over the line, but I couldn't reach them. I always fell before I got to the line."

Harriet's spells were a result of her head injury, which had probably fractured her skull and given her a concussion. But the Brodess family was sure that Harriet's spells meant she was half-witted. So they tried that much harder to sell her. But Harriet did not want to be sold and sent away from her family. And she certainly was not half-witted. She was a very clever fifteen-year-old.

Every time Mr. Brodess came to the shack with a buyer, Harriet made believe that she was having one of her spells. Or she acted very, very stupid. Her family and friends went along with Harriet's playacting. And nobody was ever interested in buying her.

CHAPTER 8:
Escape!

In time, Harriet's strength returned. She could lift huge, heavy barrels. She could pull a loaded wagon for miles. She drove the oxen in the fields and plowed from morning to night. It was said that she was stronger than the strongest man in Maryland. It was a strength she would need in the days to come.

Soon after Harriet recovered, Mr. Brodess died suddenly. Now all Mr. Brodess' slaves belonged to his son. While he figured out what to do with his father's estate, Mr. Brodess' son sent many of his slaves out to work for other people. Harriet went to work for a man named Mr. Stewart. Harriet's father also worked for Mr. Stewart, as a woodcutter. Mr. Stewart was much more fair to his slaves than Mr. Brodess was. He was impressed by how hard Harriet worked. When he hired her out to other families, he even allowed her to keep some of the money she earned. After several years, Harriet had saved a tidy sum of money.

Harriet's dream of freedom was still alive. But she had to put it off for a while. In 1844, when she was about 23 years old, she married a free black man named John Tubman. She hoped that he would help her get away to the North. But even though he was free, John's life was not that much better than a slave's. Harriet's life didn't change much either. She was still a slave, owned by the Brodess family.

John Tubman was content with his life. While Harriet dreamed of escaping to freedom in the North, the idea frightened John.

Whenever Harriet talked to John about escaping, he threatened to report her to her master. The thought that her husband would betray her made Harriet angry and sad. The marriage was not happy, and they soon parted. However, Harriet continued to use the name of Tubman.

Not long after that, word reached the Brodess slaves that many of them were going to be sold. Harriet knew the time had come to make the break for freedom. She later said, "There was one of two things I had a right to, liberty or death; if I could not have one, I would have the other; for no man should take me alive; I should fight for my liberty as long as my strength lasted, and when the time came for me to go, the Lord would let them take me."

Harriet turned for help to a white woman who lived nearby. This woman had once told Harriet, "If you ever need anything, come to me." Harriet knew that meant helping her to escape.

Without telling anyone, Harriet set out for Bucktown, where the white woman lived. When

she reached the house, Harriet said to the woman, "You told me to come when I needed your help. I need it now."

The woman gave Harriet a paper with two names on it, and directions how she might get to the first house where she would receive aid.

When Harriet reached this first house, she showed the woman of the house the paper. Harriet was told to take a broom and sweep the yard. In this way, anyone passing the house would not suspect the young woman working in the yard of being a runaway slave.

The woman's husband, who was a farmer, came home in the early evening. In the dark, he loaded a wagon, put Harriet in it, well covered, and drove to the outskirts of another town. Here he told her to get out and directed her to a second "station."

Harriet was passed along this way, from station to station. She was riding the Underground Railroad, and she didn't stop until she crossed into Pennsylvania. Now she was free at last! As she remembered years later, "When I found I had crossed that line, I looked at my hands to see if I was the same person. There was such a glory over everything. The sun came like gold through the trees, and over the fields, and I felt like I was in heaven."

But Harriet's "heaven" wasn't perfect. "I was free," she said, "but there was no one to welcome me to the land of freedom. I was a stranger in a strange land. And my home, after all, was down in Maryland, because my father, my mother, my brothers, my sisters, and friends were there. But I was free, and they should be free! I would make a home in the North and bring them there."

CHAPTER 9:
Helping Others

In the next few years, Harriet did what she swore she would do. She found work in a hotel kitchen in Philadelphia. Harriet earned a dollar a day. This was about the same amount of money she had earned when she was a slave, but now the money was all hers. Harriet also made friends with other escaped slaves. From them, she learned more about the Underground Railroad. In time, Harriet had enough information to become part of the Underground Railroad herself.

Harriet made trip after trip to the South, risking her life to bring others to freedom. She rescued her family, friends, other slaves — more than three hundred men, women, and children.

At first, Harriet just took slaves across the border into the northern states, where slavery was illegal. However, things became much more difficult in 1850, when a new Fugitive Slave Law was passed. This law said that slaves could be captured and returned to their owners even if they had already escaped to the free northern states. Freed slaves were now in danger from "slave catchers," white men who earned money by catching and returning slaves to the South.

Many slaves who had already settled in the northern states felt they weren't safe anymore. They had to leave their homes again and travel across the border to another country: Canada. Slavery was illegal in Canada, and U.S. laws did not apply there.

Harriet decided that it would be safer if she led escaped slaves directly to Canada. Although this made their Underground Railroad journey even longer, she told a friend, "I wouldn't trust Uncle Sam with my people no longer."

Harriet was loved by the slaves. They called her their Moses, because she led them through the wilderness and out of bondage. And she was hated by the slave owners, who offered a forty-thousand-dollar reward for her capture.

Harriet was never caught. She became the most famous conductor on the Underground Railroad. And, as she said, "I never ran my train off the track and I never lost a passenger." Harriet made 19 trips to the South and rescued more than 300 people.

The legend of Harriet Tubman grew during the Civil War. Fighting for the Union, she made many raids behind enemy lines as a scout and a spy. And as a nurse, she helped the sick and wounded soldiers, both Northerners and Southerners.

After the Civil War, Harriet made her home in Auburn, New York. But she never stopped doing good works. Until her death, on March 10, 1913, the woman called Moses did many things. She fought for the right of women to vote. She helped create schools for black students. She opened a home where poor black slaves could receive food and medical care. Needy people could always count on her help. She did everything she could for the poor, the old, and the helpless. At the same time, Harriet barely had enough money to support herself and her

parents, who had come to live with her after she
rescued them from slavery. She supported herself by selling vegetables door-to-door. Friends
and admirers also gave Harriet money to live.

When Harriet Tubman died, at approximately
the age of ninety-three, she was honored with
a military funeral. It was a fitting tribute to the
woman who fought so many battles for the freedom of her people.

INDEX